Paul and the Deadly Fall

Written by Suzanne Slade
Illustrated by Bill Dickson

Paul was a follower of Jesus. From sunrise to sunset, he loved to tell the good news of Jesus. Paul traveled to many cities to teach about Jesus. One night in the city of Troas, Paul taught in a small crowded room.

A young boy named Eutychus [YOO-tuh-kuss] was in the crowd. Eutychus was excited to hear Paul. But he was even more excited to stay up late. Eutychus wanted to stay up **way** past his bedtime.

There were many candles burning and lots of people in the room where Paul spoke. As the evening grew late, the room got warmer and warmer. Before long, Eutychus began to feel sleepy. "Is it time to go home now?" he asked his father. Eutychus's father shook his head. He wanted to stay with the others and hear Paul teach.

Paul shared exciting
stories about Jesus.
Since he needed to
leave town early the
next morning, he kept
talking, and talking…
and talking. Paul
taught late into the
night.

Eutychus decided staying up late wasn't as exciting as he had hoped it would be.

"Is there somewhere I can lie down?" he asked a man. The man just said, "Shhhh!" He wanted to hear Paul speak.

Then Eutychus spied
a quiet window ledge
away from the crowd.

Eutychus made himself comfortable on the ledge. A cool evening breeze blew through the window. Tiny, bright stars twinkled in the dark sky. Eutychus's eyes felt heavier and heavier.

Soon, Eutychus
fell fast asleep.

He slept so soundly,
he began to snore.
Aaah-shooo.
Aaah-shooo.

Suddenly, Eutychus
rolled off the ledge!
He fell down, down,
down from the
upstairs window all
the way to the ground.

Paul ran down, down, down the stairs when he saw the boy fall. Everyone in the crowded room rushed to help Eutychus.

When Paul and the others found Eutychus, he was lying very still. No one could wake him. He was dead.

Paul picked the young boy up and held him close. A deep sadness filled Paul's heart. But Paul trusted God, and he began to pray. He asked God for a miracle.

Slowly, Eutychus opened his eyes and stood up. God answered Paul's prayer and brought Eutychus back to life!

Paul and the others were overjoyed! They cheered and shouted, "Hooray!" Everyone thanked God for a miracle, and everyone thanked God for the young boy Eutychus.

Paul and the Deadly Fall

Life Issue: I want my child to learn that God hears us when we pray.

Spiritual Building Block: Prayer

Do the following activities to help your child understand prayer:

Sight: Play a hide-and-seek game. Choose a toy or snack your child enjoys. Hide it behind a door. Close as many doors in your house as you can. Ask your child to look for the favorite item by knocking on each door and then opening it. When your child finds the item, say, *God gives us good things when we ask.*

Sound: Look up Matthew 7:7, and point to each word as you read it. Ask, *Why should we ask God for what we need? What does God want to give us when we pray?*

Touch: Using old magazines, make a collage together of things we can pray about or ask God for. You might include pictures of food, clothing, friends, sick people, and so forth. Tell your child that God hears us when we pray and wants to give us what he knows is best.

Paul's Great Escape

Written by Suzanne Slade

Illustrated by Benton Mahan

Faith Kidz® is an imprint of
Cook Communications Ministries, Colorado Springs, CO 80918
Cook Communications, Paris, Ontario
Kingsway Communications, Eastbourne, England

PAUL'S GREAT ESCAPE
© 2006 by Cook Communications Ministries for text and illustrations

Cover and Interior Design: Sandy Flewelling

First Printing, 2006
Printed in India
1 2 3 4 5 6 7 8 9 10 Printing/Year 10 09 08 07 06

ISBN: 0781443490

God chose Paul to teach all people about Jesus. Paul talked about Jesus everywhere he went. He taught in people's homes, on the streets, anywhere people would listen.

In one town, Damascus, Paul preached in a synagogue to a group of Jewish people. "Jesus is God's Son," he said. "He is the One God sent to save us."

Many Jewish leaders became angry when they heard Paul teach about Jesus. They didn't like how popular and powerful Paul had become.

The leaders wanted to stop Paul from talking about Jesus. They didn't want more people to believe in Jesus and follow Paul.

They tried to capture Paul to keep him quiet, but Paul escaped.

Paul's friends knew he wouldn't be safe for long. The leaders were angry, so angry that they planned to kill Paul!

But Paul's friends helped keep him safe. They wanted Paul to continue telling the good news about Jesus.

The Jewish leaders in Damascus posted guards at all the city gates. The guards watched for Paul day and night. The leaders wanted to make sure Paul did not escape again.

Paul's friends were not scared of the Jewish leaders or their guards. They knew God would save Paul from his enemies, but they weren't sure how.

While the Jewish leaders searched everywhere, Paul and the others prayed. Because they trusted God, they were not afraid. They asked God to show them how to keep Paul safe.

They prayed for God to give them a plan. They asked for the perfect plan to outsmart Paul's enemies.

The Jewish leaders kept looking for Paul. They hunted for him all night long.

They were not going to stop searching until they found Paul and killed him.

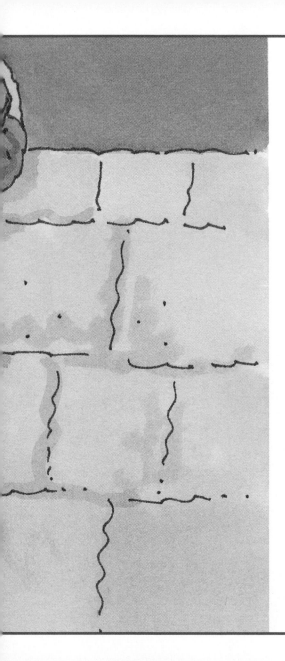

God answered Paul's prayers and showed him a way to escape. Late that night, Paul's friends lowered him over the city wall in a basket. It was the perfect plan!

God helped Paul escape from his enemies in Damascus. "Thanks be to God!" Paul shouted, as he waved goodbye to his friends. "He answered our prayers with the perfect plan." And Paul continued to preach the good news about Jesus everywhere he went.

Paul's Great Escape

Life Issue: I want my child to ask God for help.

Spiritual Building Block: Faith

Do the following activities to help your child turn to God at all times:

Sight: Look for pictures of people praying. Look in children's books, magazines, on television, in Bible storybooks—as many places as possible. Tell your child that people of all ages and shapes and sizes turn to Jesus in prayer.

Sound: Spend some time in prayer together with your child. Encourage your child to talk to Jesus just like he or she would talk to you. When your child gets stuck for words, you start talking to Jesus. Your child will love to hear your love words to God.

Touch: Show your child that we can talk to God wherever we are, whatever we're doing. Throughout the week, pray together while sitting, standing, lying down, and so forth. Pray in the car on the way to the store or as you walk to the park (with your eyes open, of course!). Demonstrate that prayer is about communicating with God and that he always hears us.

Shipwreck

Written by Diane Gardner
Illustrated by Patti Argoff

Paul was traveling by boat to Rome. "God has told me this trip will be very dangerous," Paul warned. The ship's owner wasn't afraid, even though he knew what God had said. But Paul was right.

A terrible storm came. The rain fell and the waves crashed all night. It rained and rained for days. The rain fell and the waves crashed all night. The sailors threw the cargo off the ship. Maybe then they wouldn't sink. Then, Paul heard from God again. "Don't be afraid. God told me the boat will be destroyed but everyone will make it to shore," Paul said.

One day, the boat hit a sandbar. "We're sinking!" people yelled. Everyone jumped into the water and headed to shore.

Every person made it
safely to the beach, just
as God had promised.
God had taken care of
them all.

Shipwreck

Life Issue: I want my child to learn that God will help in times of danger.

Spiritual Building Block: Trust

Do the following activities to help your child grow in trust:

Sight: Start a picture prayer journal. Each night ask your child to draw one person or event to pray for. As your child draws, ask about the picture. Discuss the best way to pray for that concern. You may want to write a short sentence or two about the prayer. Review the journal each night, and celebrate the answers to prayer. When it's full, date it and keep it as a reminder of your child's spiritual growth.

Sound: Read the dramatic story of Paul's shipwreck in Acts 27:13–44 from a child-friendly version of the Bible. Give your child a whistle or noisemaker and say, *When you hear me read about someone who was trusting God, blow your whistle.*

Touch: Use masking tape to make a boat shape on the floor. Set a box fan next to your boat and put it on high speed. Get "in" the boat with your child and read the story again.